John Owen, John Gresham, Benjamin Crosby

Gresham's Letters on the Solidity of Commercial Bills, and English Bank Notes

together with two letters to the bank directors, on the necessity of establishing a board of controul - Vol. 5

John Owen, John Gresham, Benjamin Crosby

Gresham's Letters on the Solidity of Commercial Bills, and English Bank Notes
together with two letters to the bank directors, on the necessity of establishing a board of controul - Vol. 5

ISBN/EAN: 9783337381059

Printed in Europe, USA, Canada, Australia, Japan

Cover: Foto ©Suzi / pixelio.de

More available books at **www.hansebooks.com**

GRESHAM's LETTERS

ON THE

SOLIDITY OF COMMERCIAL BILLS,

AND

ENGLISH BANK NOTES:

TOGETHER WITH

TWO LETTERS TO THE BANK DIRECTORS,

ON THE NECESSITY OF ESTABLISHING

A BOARD OF CONTROUL.

EXTRACTED FROM

" THE ORACLE AND PUBLIC ADVERTISER."

———————

LONDON:

PRINTED FOR J. OWEN, PICCADILLY; AND B. CROSBY,
STATIONERS-COURT, LUDGATE-STREET.

———

1796.

ADVERTISEMENT.

THE Public is not so easily deceived on almost any subject as that of Finance—The study of that important subject makes no part of the education either of the Scholar, the Gentleman, or the Merchant—The consequence is, that few people understand much of the matter, and those who do are seldom at the pains to write upon it; men of business are more profitably employed, and men of letters do not consider it as being in their department; thus it is that the greatest absurdities are propagated without any answer being given to them; and for the same reason it is, that when an answer is given, it ought to be in as few words as possible.

PREFACE,

ADDRESSED TO COMMERCIAL MEN.

———————

STRUCK with your apathy at a moment when your commercial exiſtence is at ſtake, I wrote the following Letters to ſhew how eaſy it is to defend your cauſe, *if you had but the will to do it*—if you felt the neceſſity. You have ſeen an alarm ſpread, that certainly influenced the Bank Directors; you have ſeen the public at large thrown into a ſtate of uneaſy ſuſpicion and doubtfulneſs; you have ſeen thoſe ravens, that croak with inward joy and outward ſadneſs, the downfall of England, ſucceed in terrifying the nation, and ſtill you have not attempted to ſpeak truth, and defend yourſelves ! ! !

Do you think that commercial wealth is intailed on your poſterity, or that its preſent poſſeſſors are invulnerable? Do you deſpiſe your adverſaries, in the ſame moment that you tremble for yourſelves, and feel the effects of their enmity? Or is it true, that what is the buſineſs of all is the buſineſs of no one? Reſolve thoſe queſtions with yourſelves and for yourſelves; I do not interrogate you for my own information.

The hiſtory of paſt times, from the fall of Tyre and of Carthage to the preſent day, ſhews that commercial wealth is the moſt fleeting of all ſublunary things, and that when once gone, it never returns again to the ſame place. There muſt be a cauſe

for

for this, and that caufe you find to be nothing
elfe than that carelefs and *avaricious* apathy
which accompanies great-wealth, againft which
poverty wages eternal war with an uninterrupted
though gradual fuccefs.

Rifen to the pinnacle of commercial greatnefs,
this is the moment of envy, and the moment of
danger; and when fo great a fabric has for its
foundation *opinion and confidence*, which are change-
able and precarious, it is fcarcely poffible to
be too much upon your guard. Could ill in-
tentioned men fucceed completely in fowing
diffidence and miftruft, thofe who have leaft
occafion for trufting others would imperceptibly
withdraw themfelves and their capitals from
trade and commerce; and thofe evils, which now
are only ideal, would at laft become real, and
thus the prophets of misfortune would have cauf-
ed their prophefy to be fulfilled.

In thefe letters, which are intentionally written
in a very brief manner, it is moft clearly proved,
that the dreaded run upon the Bank of England is, if not impoffible, at leaft improbable.
The idea of a run originated in ignorance of the
real nature of the cafe; and the Directors of the
Bank have none of thofe dangers to fear, which
have been induftrioufly held up before them.

Though a few pages are fufficient to demon-
ftrate this, yet the activity and the energy of
your enemies muft triumph, if you do not throw
off that indolent indifference, which has pro-
greffively ruined all commercial nations which
have hitherto exifted.

LETTERS

LETTERS

ON THE

SOLIDITY OF COMMERCIAL BILLS,

AND ENGLISH BANK NOTES.

———————

LETTER I.

TO THE CONDUCTORS OF THE ORACLE.

GENTLEMEN,

I HAVE obferved with a mixture of indignation and furprife, thofe attacks which have for fome time paft been made both on *public* and *private* CREDIT in this country.

The fame men who, four years ago, were occupied in diffeminating difcontent, and who aimed at deftroying the Conftitution by that means, are now attempting the fame thing by another mode. Had not the theories attached to the ruinous Rights of Man been totally unfuccefsful, thofe whofe objeƈt it is to caufe a Revolution in England, would, perhaps, have fucceeded ere now ; they can, however, have no hope of inducing people here to imitate fo fatal an example. The defire of ruining the prefent order of things, is, neverthelefs ftill as great as before;

B   and

and the mode of obtaining fuccefs is, by attacking *Public Credit*---and with it, that of all commercial men.

A defire like this, is not certainly founded on
any good will towards the nation at large: on
the contrary, it is evident, that the nation will,
in every refpect, be a lofer by fuch Revolutions
as thofe men wifh to bring on.---Their attempts,
therefore, excite indignation; but it is equally
impoffible to fee without furprife, the *cool and
indifferent manner* in which *thofe who are attacked*
behave on this important occafion.

It is well known, that *credit* depends, in a
great meafure, upon *opinion*; and it is by influ-
encing opinion, that the attack has been begun.
The effect already produced is very confiderable;
the work goes on, and is greatly favoured by
the circumftances of the prefent times. To thofe
who reflect ferioufly on this bufinefs, it muft
appear, that unlefs fome energetic efforts are
made to counteract thefe attacks, fuccefs will at
laft attend them; unlefs, indeed, fome unforefeen
event arrives, which may ferve in place of the
efforts of men.

Is it poffible that the fatal moment is arrived,
when thofe who poffefs wealth have loft the will
and the power to preferve it? Is it poffible, that
the efforts of thofe who affail the rich are fet at
nought, becaufe they come from men who have
neither

neither credit nor property themfelves? Or, what would be ftill more ftrange, do they await deftruction and ruin motionlefs and without effort, as the fafcinated traveller awaits the approach of the deftroying rattlefnake? Whatever the caufe may be, the effect is certain!!

We fee, on the one hand, great exertions making to *deftroy credit, by acting on the public opinion*; and on the other hand, we fee no efforts made to maintain it. Thofe public prints which boaft of being inimical to the Government of this country, attack the credit of the ftate and of the merchants: We fee THOMAS PAINE transformed from a fpeculator on Liberty, to a fpeculator on Finance; and what is more, his opinions, ridiculous as they are, are circulated with an *uncommon degree of induftry*. POISON IS DISTRIBUTED GRATIS, WHILE THE ANTIDOTE LAYS NEGLECTED ON THE SHELF. Thofe who are poor give a little of what they poffefs to ruin the rich; but the wealthy employ no means for their own protection. The fame was the cafe in France feven years ago. Then the Government and men of property were attacked in writings, which were circulated in a fimilar manner; but the Government and the rich defpifed opinion—they forgot that " *the fpider taketh hold with her hands, and is in King's palaces.*" We all know the fatal confequences of this ill-timed apathy; and in how

fhort

fhort a fpace of time thofe on whom the attack was made, fuffered for their indolence.

Some perfons will fay, that the cafes are not quite fimilar; they cannot, indeed, be expeƈted to be exaƈtly fo; but the conclufion is no lefs clear, that—*wherever opinion has any conneƈtion with the exiflence of a certain order of things, the efforts to change that opinion are never to be flighted.*

If a general miftruft can be infpired here in England—if the credit of Bankers is diminifhed, then our merchants can no longer give credit abroad, or make advances to our manufaƈturers at home. The trade of England would inftantly decline, and then the payment of taxes would become impraƈticable. It is thus, that by attacking Lombard-ftreet, a Revolution is attempted at St. James's; and it is on this chain of things, that the enemies of England count for fuccefs.

Our enemies would make it be believed, that becaufe the quantities of gold and filver in circulation are fmall, the circulating paper is not folid; they reprefent our Paper Credit as a bafelefs fabric about to fall; and they would therefore perfuade individuals to heap up gold, to be cautious; they give an hundred infidious exhortations, which, if liftened to, would really deftroy the mercantile fyftem. Now, Gentlemen, though I admit that the quantity of gold is not great,

I am

I am ready to prove, that no money can be more intrinfically folid than is the greateft portion of paper circulating in England, fo long as the laws and government are maintained. I mean in my next letter to enter fairly into the queftion, and expeft to convince the moft fceptical on that fubjeft, of the *real wealth and folidity, generally fpeaking, of the Banking Companies, Private Banks, and Commercial Men of England.*

GRESHAM.

LONDON,
SEPT. 11, 1796.

LETTER II.

TO THE CONDUCTORS OF THE ORACLE.

GENTLEMEN,

*T*HE *paper in circulation in England* ought to be divided into three claffes:

1ft. *Bank Paper*, or *Bank Notes.*

2d. Notes of Private Bankers; and,

3d. The Bills of Mercantile Houfes drawn upon their Correfpondents either at home or abroad.

One great caufe of the *folidity* of the paper which circulates in England, is the *ftriftnefs of the law for the immediate recovery of debts*; and another is, the *rigor of the law againft ufury.* At firft fight, any one muft perceive that the fig-

nature

nature of an individual, or a Company, bears as a mortgage upon the whole of the property of that Company or Individul, in the moſt complete manner. No legal aȼt whatever, nor any mortgage, can in its nature be more ſacred, or more ſecure, than a ſimple ſignature, by means of which the property of every ſpecies of the perſon or perſons who gave the ſignature may be ſeized, without any poſſible means of defence, or ſcarcely even of delay. In thoſe countries where the law is not ſo ſtriȼt in this reſpeȼt, paper credit never can be ſo ſolid as in England; and therefore foreigners may the more eaſily give credit to the tales that are told of a paper circulation without foundation or ſolidity.

The ſtriȼt regulations concerning the intereſt of money, which is limited to five per cent. under the penalty of three times the ſum lent, to be levied *upon the lender*, is, however, the great palladium of Britiſh Credit. As no man gives circulation to his own paper, ſo it is, that thoſe who accept of it, in order to diſcount it at ſo low a rate as five per cent. muſt be convinced of its ſolidity, becauſe the premium is too ſmall to pay *for any riſque*. Whatever paper is therefore conſidered as in any degree ſuſpicious, is cut out from circulation in the affairs on the great ſcale; and therefore the money market is always

kept

kept clear of all paper, except what, according
to the calculations of thofe who take it, is good;
and they muſt be the beſt judges, and the moſt
ſincere. Certainly, when for 1l. 5s. intereſt, a
bill of 100l. is difcounted for three months, the
man who difcounts it lays a great bet in favour
of its folidity.

When any paper gets into circulation (and
till it does we have nothing to fay to it), we
may confider that the perfon *who firſt received it
as caſh*, took every means he could to be inform-
ed of its goodnefs; that is to fay, of the probability of its being punctually paid. Experience
has always ſhewn, that the individual is generally
very clear-fighted in his own affairs; and therefore the public can have no better guarantee for
the general fafety of theirs.

After premiſing, that the ſtrict laws relative to
the regulation of intereſt, and recovery of debts,
are the main barrier againſt the circulation of
paper that is not folid, in whatever form it may
be, let us begin by confidering the three different forts of paper, taking each feparately.

Bank Notes, iſſued by Public Companies,
ought to be firſt examined; and in doing fo, we
ſhall find that they have a *double fecurity*. The
capital of the Banking Company is, in the firſt
place, anfwerable for the payment of its paper.

It

It is upon the inadequacy of this capital, that the abfurd alarms are founded.

The Bank of England, it is afferted, has only about eleven millions of capital; I fay, *afferted*, and I allow, that the capital on which dividends are paid, is not much more---but is that the REAL capital? Suppofing, however, for argument's fake, the Bank has no more, and that there are three times that quantity of notes in circulation (which is alfo afferted), does it follow that Bank Notes are not folid? No, certainly. As the Directors of the Bank *never iffue one note, except upon fome fecurity that appears to them to be good,* all thofe fecurities, as well as the original capital of the eleven millions, are anfwerable for the payment of the notes; fo that the eleven millions are not the real fecurity for the notes, but an EXTRA SECURITY; it is therefore difficult to conceive how any thing but the groffeft ignorance can throw fufpicion on the paper of the Bank.

The enemies of England fay, with truth, that there is not cafh in the Bank to pay the notes that are out. If that were not the cafe, the Bank would be an abfurd, ufelefs, and very expenfive eftablifhment. The cafh in the Bank is, however, in fuch quantity, as is far more than fufficient to pay any demand that can in the ordina-

ry

ry courfe of things occur. And as all the fecurities lodged in the Bank are at *fhort dates*, it
follows, that in cafe of any very extraordinary
run, thofe fecurities would be realized quicker
than it would be poffible to count, the fpecie
which might be demanded in exchange for the
notes.

The fecurities in the Bank are either GOVERN-
MENT SECURITIES, MERCANTILE BILLS, or
PLEDGES of INTRINSIC VALUE. The payment of
taxes is perpetually reimburfing the advances to
Government; the bills of commercial men are
either paid in Bank of England notes, or in gold;
therefore, as they become due, they either bring
back a portion of the Bank Paper in circulation,
or they bring in gold; fo that in either cafe there
is no doubt as to the folvability of the Bank.

As to the pledges of *intrinfic value*, they, our
greateft enemies, will allow, would anfwer for
themfelves.

Such then is the *folidity of the Bank* of England,
that, unlefs a general bankruptcy took place, it
could never be in any embarraffment, as it has
fecurity for every note in circulation. In my
next, I fhall enter more particularly into the
nature and folidity of this fecurity, even in cafe
of a general bankruptcy.

GRESHAM.

LONDON,
SEPT. 13, 1796.

C   LETTER

LETTER III.

GENTLEMEN,

ALTHOUGH' the paper that circulates in England is with propriety divided into three claffes; yet thofe are fo nearly connected, that it is difficult to treat of them feparately.

The BANK PAPER refts its furety, in a great meafure, upon the paper of private individuals; in confidering the folidity of the former, it is therefore neceffary to confider that of the latter at the fame time.

The only plea that has been alledged, or, at leaft, that has been admitted, as proving that the paper which circulates in England is *not folid*, is, that there is not gold or filver enough in the kingdom to pay it all off at once.' This fact I have readily admitted, and now mean to anfwer, without any fpecies of illufion or fubterfuge.

In the firft place it is to be obferved, that the very objection made to the folidity of the paper, bears with it this negative conclufion, that if there were gold and filver fufficient to anfwer for the payment of the paper, then it would be SOLID. Now it follows from the fame affertion, that if there is real INTRINSIC value of any other fort in the poffeffion of thofe who have
                                                        iffued

iffued the paper, to call it all in, then it is SOLID; becaufe all *intrinfic values* are the fame with gold and filver.

It has been afferted, and I fhall fuppofe it true, that there circulate in England 30 millions of Bank paper, and 30 millions of private notes, and that the fpecie only amounts to 25 millions —Now, Gentlemen, I am willing to allow this without any queftion, and I even go a little farther, and fuppofe that the bills and notes exceed the fpecie by 45 millions; which is 10 millions that I throw into the fcale in favour of my opponents.

I begin then with enquiring who are the perfons who have iffued thefe bills, and I find it to be the *Merchants* and *Manufacturers*, whofe whole capital, in the aggregate, is anfwerable for the payment of them. I muft therefore begin and calculate how great a value is in reality mortgaged for the payment of 60 millions of paper which is in circulation, and I find that there is property in poffeffion of commercial men to a very confiderable amount, as follows:—

$£.$

Owing by Merchants in foreign countries, all our debts being deducted, at leaft - - - -	10,000,000
Raw materials and unfinifhed goods of all forts, in the hands of Merchants and Manufacturers in Britain - - - - - - - - - - - -	14,000,000
Machines, tools, warehoufes, &c. &c. - - -	9,000,000

Manufactured

Manufactured goods in the shops, warehouses,
 furniture, &c. of people in bufinefs - - - 56,000,000
Shipping belonging to Englifh Merchants - - 10,000,000
Capital employed in Jamaica, and other poffef-
 fions abroad, belonging to Englifh Merchants 11,000,000

Property of men in trade - - 110,000,000

This is, without including landed eftates,
houfes, ready money, and other property belonging to commercial men, and thofe who have
bills or notes in circulation, all which would be
applied to the liquidation of the debt, in cafe of
a general crufh.

Thus it would appear, that there is real value.
to the amount of at leaft twice the paper in
circulation, the folidity of which is therefore
undeniable.

It may be faid, that all this property could not
come to the hammer, and be fold at its real
value; and indeed it is very true that fuch an
operation would be impoffible; but likewife it is
impoffible that fuch an operation fhould be neceffary.

The far greater portion of the Bank notes
and bills are circulating *amongft thofe very men
who have that property* So that though the property of fome individuals would come to fale,
yet as the money is owing from one to another,
fome individuals would be *receiving*, while others
were paying. As for example:---When the
private Merchants paid their bills, Bank notes

to

to the fame amount would be drawn out of circulation; fo that 30 millions of intrinfic value
would reduce the amount of paper circulation
60 millions; for the Bank notes and the private
paper are what the French call UN DOUBLE
EMPLOI; that is to fay, one million of private
paper in the Bank, and the million of Bank
paper which difcounted it, is only in reality *a
duplicate* of the fame thing; for as foon as the
million of private paper is paid, the *million of
Bank notes ceafes to exift*. Now as this is the cafe, it
follows that the 25 millions of fpecie which exift,
would draw out of circulation 50 millions of
paper; for it muft never be forgotten, in exa-
mining this matter, that the paying of the private bills reduces the number of Bank notes in
the fame proportion: fo that every bill of a
thoufand pounds paid, reduces the total circulation of paper two thoufand pounds.

The whole fpecie of the country is not indeed
in the hands of people who have bills to pay;
but more than one half of it is in the hands of
Commercial Men and Bankers; and therefore
the fpecie alone would pay off nearly one half
of the paper in circulation, and for the other half
there would remain the 110 millions as before
ftated.

Thefe calculations are not very exact, nor is
it at all neceffary that they fhould be fo; becaufe

caufe they are far within bounds, and the *furplus of
folvability* is fo great, that to be very accurate
would not be very ufeful. I fhall, neverthelefs,
on a future day, give the grounds on which
thofe calculations are founded.

GRESHAM.

London,
Sept. 17, 1796.

***

LETTER IV.

TO THE CONDUCTORS OF THE ORACLE.

GENTLEMEN,

HAVING proved undeniably the more than
fufficient means of paying all the PAPER in
CIRCULATION, without felling one-tenth part of
the property of our merchants and manufactures,
even in the cafe of a general difcredit; I am next
to confider the time in which it would be done.

Of thirty millions of Bank bills, fuppofed to
be in circulation, more than twenty millions
are in the hands of commercial men. Now as
thofe commercial men have iffued thirty millions of notes, payable in two or three months,
it follows, that they muft provide bank notes to
pay their own bills with, as they become due;
and when this operation fhall have been finifhed,
there will not remain more than ten millions of

Bank

Bank notes in the poſſeſſion of the public, and there will only remain ten millions of PROTESTED BILLS, ſuppoſing even that the commercial people have not been able to produce any gold, and ſuppoſing that the bankers had no gold likewiſe. But, Gentlemen, as it is certain, that the public and private banks have very nearly half the ſpecie in the kingdom in their poſſeſſion, it would follow that after paying the ten millions in queſtion, they would ſtill have a ſurplus of two millions or rather more.---It is to be preſumed alſo, that the mercantile and manufacturing intereſt would be able, out of their 110 millions of real property (ten of which is owing by other countries) to have realized ſomething from abroad, we may at leaſt ſuppoſe five millions--- ſo that a DELAY in paying the remaining five millions, is all that could happen in the worſt of caſes!!!

Theſe are DEMONSTRATIVE PROOFS, to which it will be difficult to find an anſwer, ſo far as they apply directly to the general maſs of notes or bills iſſued by mercantile men, or by banking companies in aid of mercantile men.

As to the individual bankruptcies that would take place amongſt commercial men, that is indeed another conſideration; but that has no connection with the affair, as it is ſtated by the enemies of England; becauſe the ſame would be

the

the cafe, even if the public banks had gold to pay all the notes that are out, and it muft ftill be kept in view, that their NOT having enough of gold is the circumftance of which THOMAS PAINE and the other enemies of England complain.

Such then is the fituation of our paper credit, fo far as Bank notes are iffued in aid of commercial men, when viewed on the great fcale---The SOLIDITY OF THE FABRIC IS INDISPUTABLE, and it belongs only to the ignorant or the malevolent to difpute it.

That portion of notes in circulation, which is iffued for the fervice of Government or the difcount of Navy or Exchequer bills, is indeed different, and it comes next to be the bufinefs to confider how fuch notes would in a moment of crifis be withdrawn.

As the advances made by Bankers to the mercantile intereft, are repaid by the bills becoming due, fo are the notes iffued to Government brought back by the taxes, which ferve the Bank as a *fecurity*: for it is to be obferved, that the Bank never lends to Government, but upon *fecurity* given for the payment. So long, therefore, as the taxes continue to be paid, the Bank is fafe.----I know that the enemies of England will here afk the fame queftion that they have been afking thefe eighty years. How long will the Government be able to pay? To this I fhall

anfwer,

anfwer, as I would concerning any individual
who has hitherto been punctual in his payments
---" Forever, if the bufinefs is well conducted;
" and if ill conducted, the diftance of time will be
" greater or lefs according to the degree of good
" or bad conduct."

I will in the moft unqualified manner maintain,
that if the affairs of this nation are wifely
managed, public credit will be kept up; but I
do not mean to fay, that if they fhould fall into
the hands of unfaithful or foolifh managers, a
Bankruptcy would not foon take place.---I fhould
not go quite fo far as the French, when upon the
eve of a general Bankruptcy they proclaimed,
that he who pronounced the word Bankrupt
fhould be infamous---I am no enthufiaft, and I
hope to efcape the appellation of empiric, as I
ftick to reafon and to fact in whatever I fay, which
every man is bound to do, who addreffes the
public on a ferious fubject.

There is yet one thing untouched upon, and
that is, thofe *bills in circulation which are not for real
tranfactions.*—Thofe, it is true, have on various
occafions been the caufe of difcredit and want
of confidence.

A Bill ought, as it bears upon its face, to be
for value received, that is well underftood, and
univerfally allowed; but it does not follow from

D   thence,

thence, by any means, that every bill which does not originate in a real tranfaction is either a bad or a dangerous bill.—A bill is, as I have already faid, a mortgage on all the perfonal property, and on the body of the perfon who figns it; and whether it originates in confequence of a real tranfaction or not, it is equally facred.

What will no doubt aftonifh many of your readers, Gentlemen, is, that if I were to have my choice of a real or a fictitious bill, I WOULD TAKE THE FICTITIOUS ONE. That I may fpeak clearly, I mean to fay that, *ceteris paribus*, the moral chances are in favour of the *fictitious bill*. —My demonftration is eafy and clear. *A.* and *B.* have had real tranfactions for a confiderable time, *B.* owes at laft a balance of 500l. to *A.* who is very glad to take the note of *B.* for the money, although he has *fome doubt* of its goodnefs, *B.* having for fome time paft been rather embarraffed. Thus it is, that bills for *real value* delivered, are frequently taken when they are *not* thought perfectly good. Had the cafe been different, and no real tranfaction had taken place, then *A.* would not have indorfed the bill of *B.* without being *perfectly fatisfied as to its goodnefs*, becaufe the tranfaction would have been entirely *optional*. It is fair then to conclude, that as the receiving fictitious bills and indorfing

them

them is a voluntary act, and as real bills are often received from neceffity, the fictitious bill is the more folid of the two!

As I by no means wifh, either by a quibble or a fubterfuge, to delude thofe who defire to ftudy this fubject, I fhall continue the fame arguments, and carry them ftill farther in my next, concerning the folidity of FICTITIOUS BILLS.

GRESHAM.

LONDON,
SEPT. 18, 1796.

―――――――

LETTER V.

TO THE CONDUCTORS OF THE ORACLE.

GENTLEMEN,

I PROMISED in my laft to extend my arguments ftill farther in behalf of *fictitious,* or as they are more properly called ACCOMMODATION BILLS.

The appellation of *fictitious* conveys a meaning which is not in this cafe a *fair one.* The bills fo called are fictitious, in fome degree, with regard to the *value received*; but they are REAL with refpect to the *obligation incurred.* Now, as it happens, the obligation itfelf, and not the caufe of the obligation, conftitutes the value of the

bill

bill in law, fo, properly fpeaking, the bill is to
all intents and purpofes a REAL and not a fictitious bill. Even the value received is not altogether a fiction in an accommodation bill;
becaufe a receipt given for the bill or the obligation, which the other party contracts, is a
valuable confideration, the fame as in any other
bargain for time, or obligation *to be* performed.

Calling then thofe bills *accommodation bills*, I
have already proved that they are in general
better than bills drawn in *order to pay debts already
contracted*.

Thofe who think themfelves very knowing in
this fpecies of negociation, will at once fay, that
I know little about the bufinefs; for that no obligations are ftronger than thofe of men who mutually accommodate each other with bills. It
will be faid, that they are fo engaged and connected, that the accommodations are by no means
voluntary, but mutually neceffary, and that in a
very high degree. This I am ready to grant is
often the cafe; but ftill it does not invalidate in
any degree my argument.

The accommodation bill may, in its origin, be
of a dubious nature; the drawer and acceptor
may be both men without credit; but if fo, they
will not find any one to difcount *their* bill, and
till it is difcounted the bill does not concern the
public.

It

It is till then a private affair entirely, and has no connexion with the general credit of the paper of the country. Before fuch a bill is difcounted, it muft have acquired, by one means or other, fuch a probable degree of folidity as to induce fome monied men to run the rifk of turning it into cafh, for the trifling advantage which the law allows.

I by no means intend to give any *general law* as being an univerfal one; on the contrary, I know that every general rule muft have *fome* exceptions; but I mean in the moft decided and unequivocal manner to maintain, that generally fpeaking, no bill that is not reckoned certain of being punctually paid can be difcounted; and till *it is difcounted, it forms no part of the fecurity for Englifh Paper Credit.*

I am well aware, that in bringing forward *new ideas* on this important fubject, I am liable to criticifm. I have already ventured upon maintaining TWO TRUTHS, that are *new* to the Financial World.

The firft is—That the private paper is only a duplicate of the Bank Notes. The fecond is what I have been this moment faying—That fictitious or accommodation bills, are, generally fpeaking, more folid than bills drawn in confequence of real tranfactions. But, Gentlemen, the truth which I have yet to hold out will feem

at

at firſt fight to be ſtill more ſtrange than either of theſe—I mean to maintain, that the scarcity of gold and silver in this country will prevent any serious run upon the Bank of England. This is indeed diametrically oppoſite to the general and univerſally received opinion; but the juſtice and truth of it will neverthelefs foon be perceived.

Let us ſuppoſe, that, from fome cauſe or other, the public became fufpicious of the credit of the Bank, and wiſhed to exchange their notes for gold. If England were not a trading country, and if the poſſeſſors of notes were *hoarders of money*, then a run upon the Bank might indeed be ruinous; but that is not the cafe.

Of the notes that are out, one-eighth at moſt circulate amongſt people *who have no concern in trade*, and no obligations to pay. Suppoſe, then, a run to begin, and that there are 32 millions of notes out, it would go on nearly as follows:—

The avenues to the Bank would be crowded with people, wiſhing to change their notes for gold; and 200, or at moſt 300,000 pounds would be changed every day. More could not be paid, becauſe the Tellers could not be able to do it with fufficient certainty.

While this was going on, the Bank would be receiving half a million of its notes every day in payment of the commercial bills in its poſſeſſion,

or

or in the poſſeſſion of bankers. So that in ten days eight millions of notes would be brought in, while the Bank would only have paid three millions in ſpecie.

The quantity of notes in circulation would, by this time, be diminiſhed *one fourth*; and a want of a circulating medium would be ſeverely felt; for a very few of the guineas received at the Bank would enter into circulation immediately. Bank notes would therefore become ſcarce, and in place of bringing them in, people would join earneſtly in demanding them, which would immediately reſtore credit, and put an end to the demand for gold.

This would not be the caſe were there gold and ſilver enough *fully to ſupply the place of the notes*, in which caſe they might all be brought in; but as a circulating medium is *abſolutely neceſſary*, it would infallibly happen, that inſtead of being brought in, they would ſoon be in greater requeſt than ever.

A run upon the Bank of England is merely a bug-bear, a phantom conjured up by our enemies, and credited by the unthinking: even the very cauſe aſſigned for that run—namely, the *want of gold and ſilver*, is the reaſon why it could not poſſibly take place.

" There is no money in the Bank," ſay our ignorant enemies---" Its cellars do not contain
" one

" one tenth of the value of the notes which it
" has issued"---Do they know (those our enemies) that the cellars of the Bank of England
may be said to extend over three-quarters of
the known world, and that half the warehouses
from Surinam to Japan would be emptied of
their goods before the notes of the Bank of
England would go unpaid.

Wherever Englishmen carry their goods (and
where is it that they do not carry them?) they
give credit, and the whole credits and property
of the mercantile people of England must answer
for their *obligations*; upon which *obligations* the
Bank Notes of England depend.---Is not their foundation sufficiently ample?

Away then far from us, those pitiful apprehen-
sions which are engendered between the malig-
nity of our enemies and the pusillanimity of our-
selves. Our paper credit is not a baseless fabric;
and as on it our commerce depends, let us
resist every attempt to destroy the one or the
other, whether coming from enemies without or
within---whether they are open or concealed
---whether they come from THOMAS PAINE, who
frankly confesses he wishes that England may be
humbled; or from a Lord or a Commoner, who
pretend to be patriots, and give their *revelations
by way of serving* their country!

It

It is not a blind confidence that is to be wifhed
for or encouraged, but that confidence which is
founded upon reafon and experience. Two
things are principally to be kept in view ; let the
Directors of the Bank confider, *that it is, their
duty and their intereft to aid commercial men, as far
as they with prudence can*; and on the other hand,
let commercial men be guided by prudence in
their fpeculations, keeping always in mind, that
they depend upon credit, and that credit depends
upon good conduct and public opinion.

GRESHAM.

London,
Sept. 20, 1796.

E ,   TO

GOVERNOR AND DIRECTORS OF THE BANK OF ENGLAND.

GENTLEMEN,

AFTER demonftrating in the foregoing letters the IMPOSSIBILITY of a RUN upon the
BANK of ENGLAND, I think it is equally my duty,
as a friend to my country, to write to you as
the *guardians* and *adminiftrators* of that *Bank*.

As *Bank Directors* you have a double duty to
fulfil---One towards the Proprietors of Bank
Stock, and another towards your country.

To underftand thofe *two* duties well, we muft
examine the original intention of the *charter of
the Bank*.

Every *exclufive privilege* has its foundation
in the public good, which is intended to be pro-
moted by it, and to which the intereft of thofe
receiving that privilege is to be *fubfervient in fuch
cafes as they are oppofite to each other*. When the
Government of the country grants an exclufive
privilege, the perfon or perfons to whom it is
granted incur the *obligation* of fupplying the
public with the article or articles for which it is
granted.

If

If this condition is not fulfilled the privilege is forfeited, as has been repeatedly determined by our Courts of Juftice, in the cafes of Patents for Inventions. I take for an inftance the Charter of the Eaft India Company; fhould that Company determine not to fend any fhips to India, or to fhut up its warehoufes, the privilege then would go to the preventing England from having any goods from India---Do you think fuch a meaning could be given to that or to any other exclufive privilege? I am confident you cannot think fo; and I am even very well convinced, that if the Company were to put an unreafonably high price upon Eaft India articles, the Charter would thereby be forfeited.

Now, Gentlemen, you are the Adminiftrators of a Company which has an *exclufive privilege* for iffuing promiffory notes; that is to fay, your Charter is fuch, that no other Company can eftablifh itfelf upon a folid and refpeftable bafis to rival you.---It is therefore, in all refpeds, *equivalent at prefent to an exclufive privilege* in the ftriéteft fenfe of the term---You will not, I prefume, fay " that you have a right to let this pri-" vilege *lay dormant*, and deprive the public of " Bank-Notes altogether." The queftion then comes to be, How far you have that right?

There is a *difcretional* but not an *unlimited* power granted to the Directors; who are not by

any

any means, at liberty to act at will with regard to the accommodation which they grant the public. I say, Gentlemen, *you are not at liberty to act in whatever manner you please,* and that you are BOUND TO ACCOMMODATE ALL SOLVENT MEN who comply with the eftablifhed and cuftomary conditions. Neverthelefs, as you may not be inclined to think fo, I fhall reafon the matter in the way that you *may* think proper yourfelves.

You will readily allow, either that *you have,* or *have not,* an unlimited power depending merely upon your own will and opinion. In fhort, the moft you can fay is, that you form a Jury, fitting upon the credit of your fellow-citizens.

My opinion is, that your power is limited; but if I am wrong in that, which is poffible, I fhall hazard the opinion, that IF you, the Bank Directors, have an *unlimited power* to refufe whatever paper you pleafe, that then the Charter of the Bank is *wrongly given;* and that the Minifter of this country does not do his duty, unlefs he does his utmoft to eftablifh a BOARD of CONTROUL for the Bank, the fame as there is for the India Company.

No power whatever (where oppofite interefts are at ftake) ought to be without fome controul. The Conftitution of thefe kingdoms has named

King,

King, Lords, and Commons, that they may controul each other--- and it was wifely done.

Shall we then have more confidence in a
Commercial Company, than in the Chief of the
Nation, who is daily controuled? The Bank
Directory alone is not to have any controul at
all. This is really too abfurd and too unreafon-
able! Even the *French Directory* is controuled;
and fhall the *Bank Directory* be like an Eaftern
Potentate, whofe word is a law as foon as
fpoken?

No, Gentlemen, if you are fufficiently unrea-
fonable to think fo, you will excufe me if I am
not foolifh enough, or complaifant enough, to
fubfcribe to your opinion.

I muft then repeat, that if your *power is arbi-
trary,* and without appeal, it ought not to remain
fo; and I will venture to give it as my opinion,
that if it fhould be proved to be fuch, the
Minifter of this country does not deferve to be
fuch, unlefs he eftablifhes a BOARD of CON-
TROUL over you; for fuch a power *as you have
is as inconfiftent with the fpirit of the Conftitution,
as it is incompatible with the interefts of the Nation at
large.*

Let us next fuppofe that your power is
limited, the bufinefs will then be to find out the
limits.

The firft affair certainly is to fupply the Public with Notes, upon fuch conditions as your
Charter

Charter permits, and as CUSTOM and EXPERIENCE
warrant.

Now, Gentlemen, as your Conſtituents, the
Holders of Bank Stock, have never ſuffered any
ſerious inconvenience, or real loſs, from diſcount-
ing, where *three ſolvable names were on a Bill*, I believe you will find it difficult to prove, that their
intereſt requires you to refuſe ſuch Bills: and I
believe, nay, I am certain, that the intereſt of
the Public requires, that the great majority of
ſuch Bills ſhould be diſcounted. I therefore do
not think that your diſcretionary power goes ſo
far, as to enable you to refuſe the major part of
ſuch Bills, unleſs (which is not the caſe) the
intereſt of your Conſtituents required you to do
ſo.

Perhaps you may ſay, that trade requires
more accommodation than your ready money in
the Bank will warrant your giving. Why do
you not then get more ready money, ſince
your Charter was given you in order that the
Public might be ſupplied, and ſince you are
bound to ſupply it? You may have more if you
will. I ſhould be glad indeed to know, what
proportion you have fixed upon between your
caſh in hand and notes iſſued; for, as it is well
known, that with the moſt ſtrict limitation of
diſcounts, you ſtill have MORE notes out than
you could convert into gold or ſilver on demand,
there ſeems to me to be NO PARTICULAR point

to ftop at, and I am indeed convinced there is none, nor can there be any.

Firft of all, it is not the fum that is out, that is the great point; you fhould take the whole fum in circulation, and multiply it by the time it is lent for; and from that you may come at fomething like a bafis for a calculation.

To make this the more clear, I fuppofe you have difcounted a bill of 1000l. at ninety days date, and another of 1000l. at ten days—By the fimple rule of calculating, you would have to preferve in hand the fame quantity of cafh in both cafes; but as the probability is, that nine times as much would come in during ninety days, as during ten—it follows then, that nine times the cafh would be neceffary.

Again, if you follow this rule, you are fubject to error ftill, though not near fo great as in the other cafe; for as the whole mafs of difcounts *increafes*, fo the *proportional fum* of cafh neceffary *decreafes*, fuppofing even *that there* is any natural proportion, which there certainly is not. The calculation then becomes a very intricate one, which I dare venture to fay no one of you ever fairly made, in which cafe you have either taken a wrong rule, or no rule at all.

It is clearly your bufinefs to provide gold and filver, if you find that it is wanted; your privilege is given you for that purpofe, and if
you

you do not do it, your privilege is in fact forfeited.

As I have already proved, that much gold and filver could never be called for, and that the payment of the bills you had difcounted would bring back the notes which you had iffued, I fhall for the prefent content myfelf with fuppofing that you have hitherto limited difcounts under the *falfe alarm of a run upon your eftablifhment*; but that idea being now done away, and proved to be groundlefs, I hope you will fhew the public that you merit to be entrufted with the direction of a National Eftablifhment upon which the profperity of our Commerce depends.

GRESHAM.

Lonpon,
Sept. 26, 1796.

TO THE

GOVERNOR AND COMPANY OF THE BANK OF ENGLAND.

GENTLEMEN,

AFTER having proved, that your duty, according to the Charter of the Bank, requires you to fupply the Public with Notes, for which purpofe your Charter was given—let us

next

next take a view of the evil, which your refusing to discount good bills produces, and we shall find it *too great to be slumbered upon*—nay, to be such as demands an *immediate remedy.*

The moment that GOOD bills cannot be discounted at the Bank, that moment every private Banker is under a necessity of limiting his discounts in a *still greater proportion* than the Bank does; because, in case of wanting money, he cannot procure it by means of the bills he has in his possession.

Each individual, in the same manner, finding himself uncertain whether he can procure money when it may be wanted, becomes hampered in his operations, and is obliged to keep *more ready money* by him than he would otherwise need to do, or than he is accustomed to do.

This cannot be better illustrated than by what happens when there is *a scarcity of bread*; each person then begins to hoard, not knowing that he can have it when wanted.

Not only then *do you hamper and plague the whole trading Nation,* but you *increase the demand for the very thing you refuse to give*; and I beg you to consider what would be the case, if at present people did not hoard up notes or cash a few days before their bills become due, in order to pay them.

You, Gentlemen Directors, are inexorable—

E   you

you have no *reafons to give*, nor will you hear
any. Your notes, and the gold which you
complain of wanting, are neceffary to pay bills,
and neither can be had in time. Bankruptcy
then takes place of ONE, TWO, THREE, and perhaps of THREE THOUSAND commercial houfes—
you ftill continuing to draw the purfe ftrings
clofer and clofer, as the danger increafes.

This, Gentlemen, is a cafe that involves the
fafety of the nation ultimately, and the profperity
of thoufands immediately.

Now I hope you will allow, that to commit
the fafety of a nation to any twenty-four men
in exiftence, let them be ever fo refpeftable, *who
are all afting on one intereft*, is rather a dangerous
experiment.

Ought any fingle intereft to be entrufted with
the YES and the NO on fo very important a queftion, particularly a YES or a NO without deign-
ing to give a reafon?

I do not wifh, in the prefent inftance, Gentlemen, to trouble you with a long letter, becaufe
you muft be allowed a little time to confider the
matter, after having feen it demonftrated, that
there is no poffibility of that run upon you for
gold, which THOMAS PAINE and fome others
would perfuade you will come; and I leave you
to confider and refleft on the juftice of what
I fay, with refpeft to the Public remedying, in
fome

fome fhape or other, your want of means, or want of will, to accommodate people who have good bills to offer.

I know you and others will fay, that the India Board of Controul is a different thing, that it was not grafted on an exifting Charter, but added at the renewal of one. Other reafons may be likewife adduced; but all thefe are done away, and more than done away, by this fingle fact, that the fafety of England is endangered, if difcount cannot be procured upon a good commercial bill, to which there are three folvable names, according to the ufual acceptation of the term—GOOD BILL.

I am not one of thofe who fay, that a Charter is only a dreffed calf fkin, with a piece of wax attached to it; but neither do I think that the *profperity of England* is to be endangered for any Charter, however facred, even if you could prove, that in refufing to accommodate the Public, you did not yourfelves deftroy your own exclufive privilege.

GRESHAM.

LONDON,
SEPT. 26, 1796.

———————

P. S. After having faid, that a little time muft be allowed to confider of the contents of thefe letters; I hope I may be permitted to add, that

if

if the fame fyftem of difcounting is without neceffity and contrary to reafon perfifted in, I fhall refume the fubjeft in a more ferious ftyle, and *awaken the nation* to the danger impending, and which I will prove to be inevitable unlefs a remedy is fpeedily applied.

FINIS.